Cambridge Experience Re

Level 4

Series editor: Nicholas Tims

Two Worlds

Helen Everett-Camplin

CAMBRIDGE
UNIVERSITY PRESS

CAMBRIDGE
UNIVERSITY PRESS

University Printing House, Cambridge CB2 8BS, United Kingdom

One Liberty Plaza, 20th Floor, New York, NY 10006, USA

477 Williamstown Road, Port Melbourne, VIC 3207, Australia

4843/24, 2nd Floor, Ansari Road, Daryaganj, Delhi – 110002, India

79 Anson Road, #06–04/06, Singapore 079906

José Abascal, 56–1°, 28003 Madrid, Spain

Cambridge University Press is part of the University of Cambridge.

It furthers the University's mission by disseminating knowledge in the pursuit of education, learning and research at the highest international levels of excellence.

www.cambridge.org
Information on this title: www.cambridge.org/9788483235669

First published 2010
20 19 18 17 16 15 14 13 12 11 10 9

Printed in Spain by Pulmen

ISBN 978-84-832-3566-9 Paperback; legal deposit: S.236-2009
ISBN 978-84-832-3563-8 Paperback with audio CD-ROM pack for Windows, Mac and Linux; legal deposit: S.237-2009

No character in this work is based on any person living or dead. Any resemblance to an actual person or situation is purely accidental.

To Fay and David Camplin

Illustrations by John McNally

Editorial management by hyphen

Audio recording by BraveArts, S.L.

Exercises by hyphen

The publishers are grateful to the following for permission to reproduce photographic material:

Imagezoo | Punchstock for cover image

Contents

People in the story

Trevor Baynham: a journalist

Safi: a schoolgirl who enjoys writing
Jay: Safi's older brother
Zoë: Safi's best friend

Freddie: a young boy who is good at football
Lucy: Freddie's cousin
Mr Crane: a football agent

Maya: a student who wants to be a teacher
Maya's father: a businessman
Janice Tucker: Maya's ex-teacher in her home country
David Morgan: Maya's teaching supervisor in England

BEFORE YOU READ

1 Look at the cover and the title. Answer the question.
What do you think the two worlds are?

Chapter 1

Different Worlds

Hello. My name's Trevor. I'm a journalist. This is a picture of me. It's what the newspaper puts on my reports. My work takes me to many different countries. I travel anywhere there's news about war or natural disasters, like earthquakes[1] and storms. As you can imagine, I've seen a lot of terrible things, both here in the UK and abroad. I try not to get upset, but it's sometimes very hard.

I want to tell you about this book. It's a book about people who have moved from one world to another. That's why it's called *Two Worlds*. Does that sound strange? Yes, I thought so. Let me try to explain a little better.

It's likely that most of us will live all our lives in the country where we were born. We may visit other countries for holidays or even in our jobs for business, but we know that we can go back home anytime we want. Sometimes it's not our decision to travel abroad, especially when we're young. Our parents may decide they want to move to a foreign country. We have to go with them, even if we don't want to. It's difficult for us to leave our friends behind. But most of us can make new friends easily and the important thing is that we're with our families. And, when we're older, we're free to make our own decisions and go back to our home country if we want to. In fact, when we're older we can choose to go to any country we want. We can go abroad for our holidays. We may even decide to study or work in another country for a while. We can choose to stay there for a long time, or even forever. We're lucky to have that choice.

There are some people, however, who have no choice at all. They have to move from their countries. Some have lost their homes. Some have lost their families. Some have to leave because of war. Some have to leave because of natural disasters. Some have paid people lots of money to travel to another country for a better life but found a much worse one instead. There are so many reasons why people have to move from one world to another. They move from somewhere they feel at home to somewhere they feel they don't belong. They leave behind friends and loving families, and move to a land full of strangers. In other words, they move from a world they know very well to one they don't know at all: two worlds.

We may see pictures of some of these people on the television or read about them in newspapers. We may feel shocked[2] or sad – but mainly thankful that it isn't happening to us. So we turn off the television or put down the newspaper and just continue our lives as usual. But we should remember that the unfortunate people we see on the television or read about in the newspapers are real people. They're ordinary people, just like you and me – ordinary people in extraordinary situations.

I've met some of them and seen how they've suffered. I report their stories on the television and write about them in newspapers. The news reports usually talk about thousands of people affected by war and millions of refugees[3]. And the television shows pictures of crowds of people escaping from terrible disasters. So it's not surprising that we can't see the separate people among the crowds, is it? It's too difficult to imagine. There are so many of these people, all with different stories. That's why I thought it was time I shared some of these stories.

I want to show the real characters behind the television pictures and newspaper reports and to allow their voices to be heard. And it's my hope that the readers of this book will remember these characters the next time they are watching or reading a news report. We should remember them and realise how lucky we are.

Two Worlds tells the stories of three young people: a schoolgirl, a footballer and a university student. Each of their stories is told in three parts: World One first introduces you to the character in their home country; the second is a news report – it's where I first meet these young people and discuss their problems or why they had to leave their homes; World Two shows them trying to get used to their new situations.

As you'll see, they all had different reasons for leaving their home country. They took different journeys to get to the UK and had different experiences when they reached here. But some things were the same for all of them. They all experienced huge changes in their lives and had to face big problems.

However, their stories also show that we human beings can be strong and that, with love and the right support[4], small steps can be taken towards a better world. You'll read a little more about that in the final chapter of this book. I have called it 'A World of Opportunities'.

Well, that's enough from me for now. I'll leave you to read the stories. Thank you for choosing this book. It shows you are interested in other people. That's a good sign. I hope it gives you lots to think about and discuss with your friends and families.

Chapter 2

The Schoolgirl

World One _____

▶ **Safi's diary**
17th March

Hi, I'm Safi. This is the first day that I've written in my diary. I'd like to write about my adventures but I don't really have any. I'm just an ordinary girl.

Today was quite an interesting day, though, because I won a prize at school. I'd written a funny poem about an elephant that forgets everything. My teacher asked me to read it out loud in class. All my friends know that I *love* elephants. I collect toy elephants – even my school bag is in the shape of an elephant – and I know a lot about them too. One thing that everyone knows about elephants is that they never forget, which is why my poem was so funny. It felt really good to hear my classmates laughing as I read my poem to them.

My teacher liked it too. She told me that I could be a writer one day if I kept practising. Then she gave me my prize. It's this diary – a five-year diary with a lock and key. Maybe I'll write all my secret thoughts in here and, of course, ideas for other poems!

My best friend Zoë was very pleased for me. She made me go to her house on the way home from school so that she could show her mum and dad the diary. (I think she wants one exactly the same for her birthday!)

Zoë's mum's an artist. She paints extremely good pictures, mostly of our village. It's such a beautiful village that it would be difficult to paint a bad picture of it, to be honest.

'Why don't I draw some pictures of your elephant?' Zoë's mum asked me. 'All good stories and poems have pictures to go with them.'

Wasn't that nice of her? Of course I said yes immediately and rang my mum to say I'd be home late for tea. I watched happily while Zoë's mum drew lots of pictures of elephants, then Zoë and I had to decide which one we thought looked most forgetful. It was so much fun that I forgot all about the time.

Before I knew it, Dad had arrived to pick me up. I heard his car outside first, then his voice shouting, 'Come on Elephant Girl. It's nearly time for bed!' I put my diary and some of the elephant pictures carefully into my bag, said goodbye to Zoë and her mum and ran out to the car.

Now I'm sitting in bed writing about my day. I didn't have any adventures, but it was exciting enough for me. I'm happy with my life. I've got great friends, a loving family and I live in a beautiful place. But I'm going to keep writing in my diary. Even ordinary girls have their secret thoughts.

12th April

It was Mum's birthday today. We had arranged a big picnic and invited lots of people from the village. We needed to keep it a secret from Mum, so Zoë's mum took her out for morning coffee. That gave us time to prepare the surprise party.

Zoë and her two brothers helped us to carry the food and drink to the park. Dad carried the tables and Zoë's dad brought the chairs. My brother, Jay, arrived late as usual and all he was carrying was his guitar and a football. 'You're not much help,' I said.

He just laughed and said, 'I'm too important to carry things – I'm a superstar!' He thinks he's so funny.

Anyway, we all worked really hard and by midday the tables were full of food and presents. We were very tired, but it was worth all our efforts to see mum's face when she arrived later with Zoë's mum. She cried when everyone shouted, 'Happy Birthday!' Why *do* mothers cry when they're happy? It's strange, isn't it?

It was a fantastic afternoon. The food was delicious, the weather stayed sunny and everyone enjoyed being with each other. Jay played his guitar and people started to sing and dance together. Then the football came out and the real fun began. The men were in two teams – young against old. As expected, the younger team won 5–0 and Jay scored three goals. I was so proud[5] of him. For me, it was the second best part of the day. The best part was the look of surprise on Mum's face when she first arrived at the picnic.

21st April

It's a lazy day today. I'm just sitting by the window looking out at my village. It looks even more beautiful than usual in this spring sunshine. The cottages look pure white between the tall green trees of the forest on one side and the big grey mountains on the other. The river looks like a bright blue ribbon. And my friends, the birds, are singing as beautifully as ever. They don't care if the sun is shining or not. They're always in a good mood. And when they're happy, so am I.

This is a friendly village as well as a pretty one. Everyone knows everyone else. Jay says that this isn't a good thing because the neighbours always notice when he gets back late at night. It doesn't matter how quiet he is when he returns home. Mum always knows exactly what time he went to bed because the neighbours tell her the next day!

5th May

Last night Mum and Dad went to a party, so I stayed at Zoë's house for the night. We listened to music in her bedroom and talked about what we were going to do when we were older. Zoë said she was going to be a singer. I said I'd write songs for her so we could both be rich and famous! We got really excited as we talked about what we'd wear, how much money we'd earn and where we'd live. We decided we're going to live together in an expensive flat and have one big bedroom each and a huge room for all our clothes and shoes.

22nd June

It was the last day of the summer term today, but I didn't enjoy it. Normally we have fun and play games and at the end of the day we sing songs together. But today the headmaster just gave us a long and boring talk in a very serious voice. He told us to be strong and he said we must remember who our true friends are. Then he started talking about politics, religion, history and other boring things that I didn't understand and wasn't interested in.

On the way home some of the boys from my class started shouting at me and some other children. They followed us home and threw stones at us. Zoë was with me when they started, but suddenly she ran away. I thought she'd gone home, but I saw her later when I went to the shops. She was standing with the same boys who had thrown the stones. I thought she must have been angry with them for hurting me, so I went to tell her not to worry.

Then, as I got closer, I saw that she was laughing and joking with them. When she saw me, she stopped laughing and we both just looked at each other as if the rest of the world wasn't there. I had a funny feeling in my stomach. I don't know why. Maybe it was the strange look in her eyes – a bit frightened, a little confused and very sad. I opened my mouth to say something, but she just turned and walked away with the boys! Why did she go with them and not stop and talk to me?

Something very odd is happening. The teachers have stopped smiling, some classmates are being mean to me and my best friend's avoiding me. 'Remember who your true friends are,' the headmaster said this morning. I thought I knew who mine were. I'm not so sure now.

24th June

Dad says we are not allowed to go out on our own. We've always got to have someone from the family with us. Jay wasn't very pleased about that!

'I don't want to be seen with my little sister!' he complained. 'It's not cool.'

He won't take me round to Zoë's house and Mum and Dad won't come with me either. I know that because I've already asked them. I just want a few minutes with Zoë to talk about what's happened. I'm sure it was just a misunderstanding.

► Letter from school headmaster to Safi's parents

12th July

Dear Parents,

The government has told all schools and colleges that we are not allowed to teach your children in the future. We have also had to take all books in your language away from the school library.

I have to ask you to keep your children away from this school until the situation changes. I advise you to do this, as it is for your children's own safety. I understand that this is very worrying news, but all schools in this part of the country now have to follow these rules.

If I receive any further news, I will contact[6] you again.

Yours faithfully,

The Headmaster

► Safi's diary

15th July

Mum and Dad got a letter from the headmaster today. Dad opened it at breakfast and his face was very serious as he read it to us.

I asked Mum where the books were now. She said that they were probably burned.

I thought she was joking, but something in her voice told me she wasn't. Surely people wouldn't burn books? That doesn't feel right. Nothing does. I wish I'd listened more carefully to the headmaster when he was talking to us all last month. I think this might be something to do with history and religion. I know it's about politics. For some reason the government doesn't like our language, but I really don't understand why.

Still, the good thing is that I won't have to go to school for a while! More time to daydream and write my poems – and maybe play with Zoë again. Yes! But Mum told me that Zoë will continue to go to school next term. 'That doesn't matter,' I said. 'I'll see her after school.' Mum and Dad gave each other a strange look and Dad said that I probably wouldn't see Zoë and her family again, as 'they are different from us'.

That made me very angry. I shouted at my dad, 'When did they become "different from us"? They're our friends. Zoë's like my sister. I'm going to write songs for her. We're going to live together when we're rich and famous. What has changed? Why can't I see them?'

I was so angry that I ran to my bedroom and cried for ages. Mum and Dad were wrong to talk about Zoë and her family like that. I knew they were wrong. But a little voice kept whispering in my head, 'Why did Zoë avoid me? And why didn't she help me when the boys were throwing stones at me?'

2nd August
Everything has changed. My dad looks worried all the time and my mum hasn't smiled for weeks. They both look very tired. I know they aren't sleeping because I hear them talking to each other during the night. I've stopped asking, 'What's wrong?' because they just reply, 'You're too young to understand.' Why do adults say this to children? Why don't they help us to understand instead? We're not stupid. We know something terrible is happening. It's worse for me too because we writers are very sensitive[7] people.

I can still only go out when Jay is with me. We both hate that. I love Jay very much, but I'd much rather be with Zoë.

We walked past her house yesterday. She was looking out of her bedroom window, so I waved at her and for one wonderful moment she looked really excited and waved back at me. Then her face changed, as if she'd just remembered something awful. At that moment, her dad's face appeared at the window and he quickly pulled the curtains shut.

I asked Jay to wait with me because I was sure that Zoë was going to come down and say hello.

'Don't waste your time, Safi,' Jay said. And he was right – she never came.

As we turned away, we saw one of Zoë's brothers. Jay immediately put his arm around me. I couldn't understand why at first. But then suddenly Zoë's brother started to shout at us. He used some really nasty words. I was so shocked that I couldn't stop shaking.

Jay pulled me closer to him and whispered, 'Just keep walking, Safi. We'll soon be home.' We walked as quickly as we could and all the time I could hear Jay's calm voice telling me everything was going to be OK. That's when I changed my mind about wanting to go out alone. I was so pleased that Jay was with me.

When we got home, he put his hands on my shoulders and his eyes were dark and serious. 'The adults are teaching the children to hate, Safi. There's danger everywhere, but I'll always be here for you. Remember that.' Then he hugged me. Jay hugged me! He's never done that before. Now I know that things are bad.

10th September

Mum and Dad are frightened. I can see it in their eyes. They've packed a suitcase and they keep it by the kitchen door. Mum told me to put some of my favourite things in a bag 'in case we decide to go on holiday'. Holiday? Does she think I'm stupid?

My village is silent and there's electricity in the air. It feels like the night before a storm …

Love your neighbour

By Trevor Baynham

 I'm writing this report from a refugee camp. I've been to many places like this during my time as a reporter. I should be used to them ... but I'm not. Every time I visit a camp I am shocked by the noises, the smells and the terrible confusion and helplessness all around me.

Refugee organisations have recently complained about the unhealthy conditions in some camps. This seems to be one of those camps. Despite the efforts of the people working here, there is hunger, illness and exhaustion everywhere I look.

There are thousands of people here and not enough space, food or drink for them. The situation is getting worse every day, as more and more people arrive. Everyone has to queue up for hours just to get a bowl of watery soup, some bread and a small can of water.

Journalists are a bit like detectives. We ask lots of questions beginning with Who? Where? Why? What? When? and How? We're trained to ask questions and find answers.

In situations like this I always ask, 'Who is living here? Where did they come from? Why did they leave? What happened to them? When did they arrive? How did they get here?' I try to avoid the unhelpful question that some journalists ask, which is, 'How do you feel?' The answer is obvious for anyone to see.

Soon after arriving here, it became clear that there was something very different about this camp. There are very few boys. I know that there are usually more female refugees than male – the women often escape with their children while the men are fighting. So it is not unusual to see fewer men in camps. But why are there hardly any boys here? This was just one more question I needed to ask.

The written words in news reports are sometimes not quite powerful enough to tell people's stories properly. So I've left the words of one woman I interviewed largely unchanged. Maybe when you read her words, you'll understand the feelings of confusion and helplessness I mentioned earlier.

'Is he a journalist?' the woman asked the interpreter[8] when she saw my notebook and microphone.

'My daughter wants to be a writer when she grows up. Say hello to Mr Baynham, Safi. He's a journalist.'

I smiled at the little girl beside her, but she just stared up at me with dark and frightened eyes. She was holding onto her mother's arm with one hand and a big toy elephant with the other.

'Please tell her not to be frightened,' I said. 'I only want to ask a few questions.'

'I'll answer your questions,' said the woman. 'The world must know what has been happening in our country. But my daughter ...' She paused and looked down at the little girl. 'She has only said a few words since we left our village.'

'What has been happening?' I asked the woman.

19

'Our neighbours attacked[9] us. We'd lived peacefully together for years but suddenly things changed. It started when my children weren't allowed to go to school any more. Then our churches were closed down or destroyed. Soon our farms and businesses were being taken away from us, then ...'

She stopped talking, closed her eyes and lowered her head, as if the memories were simply too heavy. When she spoke again, her voice was so full of sadness and pain that I felt guilty for asking the question.

'My life is over. I can't believe our neighbours did this to us. The man whose daughter used to play with my daughter came to our house with his sons. They took my husband and son into the forest. And they killed them. We could hear the noise of the guns – pop-pop-pop – in the distance and we knew what they were doing. We thought we were going to die too. I ran into the house and quickly took a suitcase. My daughter only had time to take her school bag. We ran away as fast as we could and as far as we could. Then, when we thought the danger was over, we walked. And we walked.'

She paused and pointed to the crowds, the mess and the madness around us.

'It took us days to get here. I don't know what's going to happen to us now. We had a beautiful house, but now we are living in a tent. We had good jobs and enough to eat. Now we're always hungry and have to wait for other people to give us food. We had a normal and happy family life. Now it's just me and my daughter.'

I asked her if she knew why these terrible things had happened in her country. She shook her head.

'No, I don't understand. These people were our friends. We went to each others' weddings. Our children went to school together. We laughed and we cried together. Then suddenly our friendship and love changed into hate. Why? Is it just because we speak a different language and follow a different religion? It was never a problem before, so what changed? I don't know. I'll never understand. Never.'

Then she put her head in her hands and started to cry.

'No more questions please,' said a little voice by my side, 'My mum's tired.'

The daughter was talking again. I turned to reply, but then I saw again the darkness and fear in her eyes.

'No more questions,' I agreed and slowly pushed my way through the crowds with my interpreter to interview more people.

After a minute, I turned and looked back. The woman and her daughter were sitting together in the mud. The young girl had her arms around the woman and was holding her close, just like a mother would hold her child.

War brings many changes. Sometimes children have to become adults. And adults become little children again.

World Two _____

▶ **Safi's diary**
17th March
It's been exactly one year since I first started writing in my diary. So many things have changed. I'm living in London now and I hate it. It's dark, grey and ugly. Everyone's in such a hurry that they never have time to stop and smile. They certainly don't have time to notice a little girl like me.

The interpreter at the airport said we were lucky to be here. The British government has decided to allow us to stay here for a while until things get better in our own country. She said this would be our home for a while.

Home? How can I feel at home here? Where's my forest? Where's the river? Where are my mountains? There are no pretty birds singing happily in the trees, just dirty old pigeons sitting on tall buildings and looking bored.

I didn't want to come here. I wanted to go home. I

dreamed about my village all the time I was living in that horrible camp. Sleep became my way of escaping from the camp because my dreams were so much nicer than the real world. I thought if I dreamed about home enough it would become a reality, but I was wrong. This is my reality now – living in a hotel with lots of other people from my country.

Anyway, at least I've got a proper[10] room to sleep in again. I'm sharing with Mum, of course. We need to stay together. But the strange thing is that now I can't sleep at all. Every time I close my eyes I feel like I'm in the camp again and the smells and noises come back and fill my head. I could escape from the camp while I was living there but now that I've left, its ghosts visit me at night and keep me awake.

I want to tell Mum about my nightmares, but I don't want to make her feel any worse than she does already. Night time is the only time she gets any peace, unlike me. During the day she just sits in her chair and cries. I try to look after her, but I really wish somebody would look after me. My brother, Jay, said he'd take care of me. He told me he'd never leave me. He promised.

20th March

Today was the first day at my new school. Everyone was looking at me but not in a friendly way. I thought a couple of girls were smiling at me, but they were laughing at my elephant bag. They think it's a toy, but they don't understand. I know it looks childish, but it reminds me of home and I'm always going to carry it with me.

Some of the children did try to talk to me, but I couldn't understand what they were saying. English is a strange language. It's like listening to music that you don't like. The teacher seemed kind, but I couldn't understand him either. Every few minutes he stopped talking and looked at me as if he wanted me to reply to a question. How could I give an answer when I didn't know what the question was? But he kept looking at me and pointing, so I pointed back. Everyone laughed.

The last time I heard laughter in the classroom it was fun. This was a different kind of laughter. It was nasty. I wanted to run away and cry. But I didn't. I wouldn't. I haven't cried since I left my village. I haven't cried for my dad or my brother, so I will NOT start crying just because of those silly kids at school.

► **Note from Safi's teacher to headmistress**

5th April

Just thought I'd leave you another note about Safi. She's still very unhappy and doesn't mix with the other students in my class. I know that her progress is likely to be slow, but she's not improving at all. In fact, she's getting worse. Last week, for example, she hit another girl just because she touched her school bag. I'm very worried about her and thought I ought to let you know.

I know you've already contacted a number of refugee organisations for help and you're waiting for replies. While we're waiting, I thought it would be a good idea to arrange extra English classes for Safi. What do you think?

I'm sure that if her English improved, she could start to make friends and feel more at home here.

Jack Brown

► **Safi's diary**

12th April

I wished Mum 'Happy Birthday' this morning and gave her a card, but she wasn't interested. I'm worried about her. She's not getting any better. The doctor has given her lots of medicine, but it just makes her sleep all the time.

When she's not sleeping, she's crying. I keep telling her that everything's going to be all right, but I don't think it is.

I sometimes feel like crying myself, but I have to be strong. I'm also afraid that if I start crying, I'll never stop.

30th April

I've started going to a special class three times a week in a local community centre[11]. I'm learning English with other children from different countries. None of us speaks English very well yet, but we all help each other.

My English teacher's a lovely lady. She's kind and patient and always seems to know the right things to say to us. I'm learning quite quickly because she makes me feel confident.

All the students are trying really hard. I think it's partly because we all speak different languages. So if we don't speak English, we won't get to know each other! Sometimes, though, we don't need to talk at all to understand each other. We've all had bad experiences. It shows in our eyes. Yes, our eyes speak louder than our voices.

4th May
Mum's a little better, I think, but she's still sleeping a lot. Sometimes when she wakes up, she doesn't know who I am. I think it's because of all the medicine that she takes. But it still makes me feel very frightened. I'm worried that she's lost in a world of her own – a world where I can't reach her.

I'm living in a strange country. I'm speaking a strange language. And now I feel like I am living with a stranger too. It's as if she's the child and I'm the mother. It's not fair. *I* want to be the *child* again.

12th May
A new boy joined our English class today. He's called Freddie and he came to this country on his own. He lives in a house with lots of other boys. He's got no family here at all! He says that there are adults in the house who look after him, but it's not the same as having your parents with you, is it? I thought things were bad for me, but at least I've got my mum. I know she's ill, but she's still my mum. For the first time since I arrived here, I feel luckier than someone else.

Freddie's older than me, but I feel comfortable with him. He says he feels the same way about me. It's nice to have someone to talk to, even though we have to do it in English!

5th June
Freddie's like a best friend and a brother in one person. Obviously, I can't talk to him about clothes and make-up like I did with Zoë. And he'll never be like Jay. Never. But he does

look after me and jokes with me like Jay used to. He says I've got a terrible English accent, so I tell him that he can't spell! When I'm with Freddie, I feel like I'm a child again, and it's been a long time since I've felt that way.

He isn't rude about my elephant bag though, because he knows how much it means to me. He knew immediately that it was an African elephant, because it's got big ears. He says he'd see them near his village sometimes. Wow! I wish elephants had visited my village!

I can share my thoughts with Freddie and he seems to understand. I've told him about my dreams of being a writer and he's shared his dreams about being a footballer. He was surprised that I knew so much about football. I told him that I had to learn when I was very young, or Jay and me would have had nothing to talk about!

Freddie invited me to watch him play football this afternoon. He'd told me he was good, but he's even better than that – he's brilliant and I told him so.

'I know,' he replied, 'I'm a superstar!'
He thinks he's so funny!

11th June

I've just won another prize … for my English! Actually, we all got the same prize – an English dictionary – but for different things. I got mine for 'Best Accent' and Freddie got his for 'Best Spelling'.

We couldn't stop laughing. Our teacher didn't know why, but she laughed with us anyway.

I ran home to show Mum my dictionary, but she was in bed, as usual. She tried to look interested, but I could see that she just wanted to sleep. Poor Mum. I thought my prize would cheer her up, like my writing prize did last year. She was so excited for me then, but now …

NO! I mustn't do this. I mustn't stay in the past. My teacher told me it's very important to remember the past but not to stay there. She says we should try to see the past as another world – 'Yesterday's World'.

'You can visit "Yesterday's World",' she said. 'You can always visit it. Sometimes it will be a good visit. Sometimes it will make you sad. If you feel sad, you should come back to 'Today's World'. Then try to think about one or two good things that have happened to you here.' She calls them 'happy thoughts'. She also said that if we can't think of any 'happy thoughts' we should visit 'Tomorrow's World' where we can dream of doing anything we want.

She knows I'm a writer and I've told her about my diary, so she says I should write my 'happy thoughts' in here, as well as my sad ones.

So, can I think of two good things that have happened today? My prize. Freddie's prize. Laughing so much that my stomach hurt. Wow, that's three things!

8th July

It's Freddie's birthday next week. I asked him what he was going to do.

'Nothing,' he said. 'It's not the same without my family.'

I hated to see him so sad, so I quickly invited him to spend the afternoon with me and Mum.

He wasn't sure at first, but finally agreed. 'What are we going to do?' he asked.

Do you know, I hadn't actually thought about that? I just thought it would make him happy – and maybe Mum too. Who knows?

9th July

I told Mum about Freddie's birthday, but she just looked even sadder than normal. I was so disappointed. I'd tried to make things better but, as usual, I'd just made things worse.

But a few hours later I noticed that she was writing lists on a piece of paper.

'We need a cake,' she said, 'and some sandwiches and music. Oh, and you must talk to your English teacher, Safi, and see if we can use the community centre.'

I couldn't believe it. She was starting to sound really excited!

'Do you remember my surprise party last year, darling?' she said. 'You made me feel so happy. Well, Freddie doesn't have anyone here to do that for him, does he? So *we*'ll have to be his family and make his birthday as happy as mine was.'

Then she gave me a big hug and said, 'Thank you for looking after me, Safi. You've been very strong, but it's time I started being your mum again and looking after *you*.'

One 'happy thought' is enough for today. I've got my mum back!

15th July

Freddie's birthday – what a fantastic day! When I went to collect him, I could see he was excited.

'What did you buy me?' he joked.

'Nothing,' I replied and tried very hard to look sorry.

'Don't apologise, Safi,' he said. 'I know you haven't got any money.'

'I didn't *buy* anything, but I'm *giving* you this!' I laughed and gave him … my elephant bag. He didn't want to accept it at first.

'But you brought this from your country! I know how much it means to you!' he said.

'And it reminds you of your country too, Freddie, so I want you to have it,' I replied.

I don't expect him to use it. It's not that kind of present. He knows it's not just a bag in the shape of an elephant. It's so much more than that. I think he's probably the only person in the world that understands. And he needs it more than me, you see. I've got my mum here, but his mum's far away.

We walked to the community centre in a friendly silence. When we got there, my mum ran towards us with a big smile on her face. 'Happy Birthday, Freddie!' she said.

She led him into the big hall, which was absolutely full of people. There was food and drink on the tables and a big pile of presents on one of the chairs.

Freddie spent a long time looking around him without saying a word. Then he whispered something to my mum and his shoulders started to shake. Oh dear. This isn't what I'd expected. He was crying! Mum quickly put her arms around him and hugged him tightly, just like she used to hug Jay. They stayed like that for a long time. I became even more worried when I saw that Mum was crying too. Maybe this party wasn't such a good idea after all.

But then somebody put some lively music on and everyone shouted 'Happy Birthday!' Mum used her handkerchief to dry Freddie's tears, then gently touched his hair and smiled.

'It's time to stop crying and start enjoying ourselves,' she said.

LOOKING BACK

● ●

1 Check your answers to *Before you read* on page 4.

ACTIVITIES

● ●

2 Complete the summary of Chapter 2 with the words in the box.

Safi (x3)	Jay	headmaster
parents	mum	Zoë (x2)

¹ _Safi_ lives with her parents and brother, ² _____ . Her best friend is ³ _____ and their families are good friends. On Safi's ⁴ _____ 's birthday, everyone arranges a surprise picnic to celebrate. Safi's family and ⁵ _____ 's family have a wonderful time together. But on the last day of school term, everything changes. Some boys from ⁶ _____ 's class throw stones at her. Safi's ⁷ _____ sends a letter to ⁸ _____ 's parents to say that she isn't allowed to go to school. Safi doesn't understand what is happening, but suddenly Zoë's ⁹ _____ won't allow Zoë to speak to her any more.

3 Are the sentences true (*T*) or false (*F*)?
1 Safi's funny poem is about a tiger. ☒ F
2 Because of the situation, children are not allowed to go out alone. ☐
3 Safi is doing extremely well at her new school. ☐
4 Freddie loves joking with Safi. ☐
5 Freddie's birthday party is held at Safi's home. ☐

4 Match the two parts of the sentences.

1 Safi likes elephants [c]
2 Zoë spends time with some boys ☐
3 Safi doesn't enjoy her new school ☐
4 Safi thinks that Freddie's party isn't a good idea ☐

a because she cannot understand English.
b when she sees him crying.
c because everyone knows that they can remember things.
d although they behave in a bad way towards her best friend.

5 Answer the questions.

1 How do Safi's neighbours change?

....

2 What does Safi take with her when she leaves the village with her mum?

....

3 Where do Safi and her mum go after they run away?

....

4 Compare Safi's life in her home country and in London.

....

LOOKING FORWARD
· ·

6 Tick (✓) what you think happens in the next chapter.

1 Freddie's parents ask him to return to his home country. ☐
2 Freddie becomes a famous footballer. ☐
3 Freddie starts a football team at the community centre. ☐

Chapter 3

The Footballer

World One _____

▶ Freddie's school essay
2nd April

My Dream

My name's Freddie. I live with my mum and dad in a small village. My dad works in a local market and my mum mends clothes.

When I leave school, I'm going to work with my dad. I already help him at weekends. It's very hard work and he needs a strong boy to help him carry things.

I'm strong, it's true. I'm not very good at writing, but I'm stronger than most boys in my class. I read quite slowly too, but I can run faster than any other boy in my village. And when I'm kicking a football along the dry, hard ground in my village, I'm the happiest boy in the world.

I love football. It's my dream to be a professional football player and maybe play in Europe one day. When I think about this, I get very excited. My heart starts beating really fast. I don't feel like that when I think about working in a market. But I suppose that's the difference between dreams and reality, isn't i ?

ot that I want to be rich and famous. I just want to
ˈ with the best players. But, of course, if I had lots
ˈd look after Mum and Dad. I could buy them
ˈr wanted and they wouldn't need to work
ˈ them a house in town near my cousin,

Lucy. Her dad works in an office there and he's got a very nice house with a colour television, computer and telephone. And he's got a car! Mum and Dad have none of these things.

I'm in the school football team. We're called The Cheetahs. Cheetahs are strong and fast, you see, and so are we. I've scored twenty goals already and we're only halfway through the season. My dad always comes to watch me when I play.

A man called Mr Crane has started to come and watch my games too. He's a football agent[12]. He finds football players for big clubs around the world. I see Mr Crane talking to my dad. I don't know what they're talking about, but I hope Dad's telling him that I'm a good player! Mr Crane is a very rich man who owns lots of football academies here and abroad. They're a type of school for training young football players. He's got an academy somewhere in Europe. I've heard that this is where he sends the best young football players. Maybe I'm closer to my dream than I thought. Maybe Mr Crane is interested in me and will send me to one of his academies. This would be my dream.

► **Letter from A1 Football Academy to Freddie's parents**

5th May

Dear Parents,

My name is Mr Crane and I am Director of the A1 Football Academy. It is one of the most successful football academies in the world. We are always looking for good young footballers so that we can help them to achieve their dreams of playing professional football.

I am writing to you because I believe that your son could achieve that dream. I have been watching him over the past month and I know that with the right training, he could play for a professional team in Europe one day.

Your son is a natural footballer. He should have the opportunity to show the world how well he can play. And, as I am sure you realise, professional football players can earn a huge amount of money. Please think carefully about this letter and your son's future.

You can contact me on the mobile number below. I look forward to talking to you in the near future.

Yours sincerely,

E Crane

Director

► **Letter from Freddie to his cousin Lucy**

10th June

Dear Cousin Lucy,

I'm so excited. Mr Crane and his football academy are interested in me! He came to The Cheetahs' football practice today and told me all about his academies. He has hundreds of people working for him, both in this country and in Europe. He knows some very important people. He asked me who my favourite football players were and he's friends with most of them!

He told me that he's already written to Mum and Dad about me. It's odd that they didn't mention it to me. Anyway, he gave me another letter and told me to give it to them when I got home.

He also said that if I practise hard, I could probably be a footballer in a top European team in a few years! Can you imagine? Me – a famous footballer? It's all I've ever dreamed of. I was so excited, I couldn't wait to give Mum and Dad the letter. In fact, I ran home so fast I could have overtaken a real cheetah!

I gave Dad the letter and he read it very quickly, then passed it to my mum. They didn't seem very excited. Mum smiled at Dad, but it wasn't a big smile. Dad started writing numbers on a piece of paper, then he told me to go to my room because he and Mum needed to discuss a few things.

► **Letter from A1 Football Academy to Freddie's parents**

8th June

Dear Parents,

Thank you for calling me this morning. I was disappointed to hear your decision about Freddie.

This is a great opportunity for your son. He is a brilliant footballer and I know that you want the best for him. With my help he could be one of the greatest footballers in the history of the game. Do you really want to stop him from following his dream?

I understand that you are worried about the amount of money we ask for our services. Let me explain the costs again. The 3,000 euros will pay for passports, visas and air tickets, plus hotels when we arrive in Europe. It also includes a year of teaching and accommodation at one of our academies. Of course, you are also paying for my advice and help as the director of the organisation.

I am sure you will agree that your son's future is worth spending this money on. But, just in case you still have any worries, I have attached copies of some letters we have received from parents who are very pleased with our services.

I know you love your son very much. I am asking you to put your trust in me so that I can help him to be the best footballer he can be.

Yours sincerely,

E Crane

Director

► **Letters from Freddie to Lucy**

17th June

Dear Cousin Lucy,

Mum and Dad have begun to act very strangely since I gave them that letter. Sometimes I hear them shouting at each other, but as soon as I walk into the room they stop. Then they wait until they think I'm busy doing my homework and continue their conversation in whispers.

Your dad drove all the way to our house last night and I heard him talking to Mum and Dad about money. I'm sure your dad told them that he was going to try to get hold of 3,000 euros. But I must have made a mistake. That's a lot of money, isn't it? Maybe we'll have to pay Mr Crane *some* money for me to go to his academy, but it can't be thousands of euros, can it? No, I've definitely made a mistake.

Freddie

15th July

Dear Lucy,

I really enjoyed my birthday party. Thank you for coming. I didn't realise that so many people were interested in my

dream of playing football! It seems that everyone in the village has given my mum and dad some money for my training. This money is the most generous birthday present I've ever had in my life! I made sure that I said thank you to everyone. But please, thank your dad again for organising everything. I'll pay everyone back, I promise. Because I know – I just know – that one day I'm going to be a successful footballer.
Freddie

25th August

Dear Lucy,

Well, my big adventure starts next week and I can't wait. Well, actually, I feel a bit frightened. The farthest I've ever travelled before is to your town. So flying to another country seems frightening.

Mum told me last night that it's normal to feel nervous when you're going to do something new. Then she smiled and gently touched my hair, like she used to do when I was a small

boy. When she hugged me, I could feel her body shaking. She said she was cold, but I think she was crying because when I looked up, her face was wet. I know she's going to miss me and I'm going to miss her too. I'll miss you all very much, but I'll think of you often.

Mr Crane says he can't travel with me as he's very busy, but he says that one of the best men he has will come with me on my journey and take me to the academy. I feel like a star already!

Love,
Freddie

World Two

▶ Postcard from Freddie to his parents

3rd September

Dear Mum and Dad,

Well, I've arrived! It was a very long journey and I'm *very* tired. But it's all very exciting. The taxi journey to the hotel was amazing! Every building in the city was lit up and it looked magical.

My hotel room is lovely and I have my own bathroom! I can't wait to have a long, hot bath then climb into my comfortable bed. But before I do, I want to finish writing this card and put it in the postbox. Mr Crane's friend bought me some postcards and stamps. He told me to write to my family and tell them that I've arrived safely. He's just gone to the academy for a meeting.

He told me to get a really good night's sleep as I've got an important day ahead of me tomorrow.

Love you,
Freddie

► **Letter from Freddie to Lucy**

4th September

Dear Lucy,

You mustn't tell anybody what I'm telling you now. I think I'm in big trouble.

Mr Crane's friend hasn't come back for me. I don't know where he's gone and I don't know how to contact him. I don't have his telephone number and I only know his surname. I think he gave me a false name.

Lucy, I think that Mr Crane might be a criminal. I'm worried that he's taken our family's money and run away. I'm not even sure that there is an A1 Football Academy. I'm starting to think that he lied to us.

I waited all day for Mr Crane's friend today. Then the manager of the hotel told me I had to leave or pay for my room for another night. I don't have any money, of course. So now I'm alone in a big city and I don't know what to do or where to go. I've never been so frightened in all my life. I need to share my fears with someone. Please be a strong girl and keep my secret.

I can't send you a postcard because anyone could read it. So I took some hotel writing paper and envelopes before I left and I'm using them instead. You can tell your mum and dad you had a letter from me if you want but, please, don't tell them what has happened.

I need some time to think. I'll write again very soon.
Love,
Freddie

Football can be a dangerous game

By Trevor Baynham

 There are thousands of homeless young people all over the world. We've all seen them. During the day they walk around, carrying their blankets and a bag.

Sometimes they sit on the blankets and sell cheap souvenirs to tourists or they beg – they ask for a few coins to buy something to eat. At night, they sleep in blankets, outside shops or in parks.

You may have sometimes asked yourselves why they live like that. You may wonder why they don't have a home – like you and me. Well, some of them do have homes. They just can't get back to them. Today I'm going to write about some of those young people whose homes are thousands of miles away.

There are many reasons why the young become homeless. One of these reasons is football. Well, it's the dream of playing football, actually. Some boys arrive in Europe because they are hoping to play for one of the big football clubs. Sadly, their hope soon dies.

Most of them are quite good footballers. Many of them have met a football agent in their countries – a man who said he had a number of successful international football academies. The agent probably told them he knew some famous football players or even managers. He probably told the boys' parents that their child was the best footballer he had ever seen. He then persuaded the families to pay him thousands of euros so he could train the boys. He promised that one day their sons would be successful, rich and famous.

But these 'agents' are not what they seem to be. They don't have any important friends in the football world. They don't intend to train the boys. Most of them don't even have an academy at all. They take thousands of euros from poor families and keep the money for themselves.

And what happens to the boys? They suffer very badly. They travel to another country and are left there on their own. Some fly with the 'agent' on a one-way ticket. When they arrive, the agent takes them to a hotel. They spend one night there and then the agent disappears. Suddenly they are alone. Some boys even start their journeys on their own. They travel to the foreign country, sometimes in crowded boats. But when they arrive, there is no one to meet them.

These boys are lost in a strange country and they can't get home. Most of them have no money at all. Many of them do not even speak the language of the country they are now in. They've only got short tourist visas or no visas at all. So soon they are in the country illegally[13].

Heartless men who know that they can make money out of the dreams of innocent young boys and their parents are to blame for all this harm.

I spoke to one boy today. He was selling cheap jewellery on a street corner.

'I left my home three months ago,' the boy said. 'I was so excited about my new life in Europe. I remember the taxi ride to the hotel. Everything looked so different and exciting. And my first night in the hotel was fantastic.'

The boy closed his eyes. He seemed to be in another world, as he remembered all that had happened.

'The bed was so big and the sheets were clean and white and there was a little bar of chocolate on the pillow. Oh, and I had my own bathroom.'

He stopped talking for a minute and smiled weakly.

'I remember everything about that hotel room. I thought that this was the beginning of a wonderful new world for me. I was going to become a famous footballer and earn more money than I could ever imagine. But I was so wrong. Look at me now.'

The boy looked down at his torn jeans and old T-shirt.

'I'm dirty and poor. During the day I sell jewellery to tourists and at night, I sleep on the street.'

He showed me a pile of leather bracelets at his feet.

'Do you make much money?' I asked him.

'Not much,' he admitted. 'That's why I sometimes have to beg people to give me some money instead. If my mum and dad could see me now ...'

His eyes filled with tears and his head dropped.

'Have you spoken to them since you left home?' I asked.

He shook his head, 'No. I sometimes write to them but I just tell them lies. They think I'm happy.'

The boy suddenly looked up at me. 'But I don't think I'll ever be happy again. How can I be? I haven't got a visa to stay here or any money to go home. I'm so frightened that every time I see a policeman I run away. I was always such a good and honest boy at home. My mum would tell you that.'

As soon as he mentioned his mum, the boy started to cry. Then, to my surprise, he suddenly took my hand and asked, 'Do you live here? Could I stay with you for a few days? Could you help me, please?'

I told him I was only visiting and that I was flying back to the UK later that day.

The boy suddenly looked embarrassed. 'I'm so sorry. I shouldn't have asked you,' he said, 'Thank you for listening to my story.'

He smiled bravely as he shook my hand, but I could see the fear in his eyes. His apology had already made me feel terrible, but his false smile simply broke my heart.

At that moment, the police arrived and the boy quickly picked up his blanket and started to collect together the few coins he had in front of him. I could see that he was going to run away again. I don't know why I did it, but I quickly pushed some money and my business card into his hand before he disappeared back into the crowds.

I know it was very unprofessional of me to give the boy money, but I felt so sorry for him that I just wanted to help him in some way. For one moment I totally forgot about being a journalist and staying detached. Sometimes it's hard to find the balance between being professional and just being human.

▶ **Postcard from Freddie to his parents**

20th December

Dear Mum and Dad,

Happy Christmas!

I'm sorry that I haven't written for a long time, but life at the academy has been so busy. And our football coach doesn't want us to contact our families too often during the first year. He says we need to keep our minds on football.

But we're allowed to relax sometimes. We've all come to England for our Christmas break. It's very cold! Everyone is shopping for Christmas presents. I miss you all so much, but please don't worry about me. I'm having lots of interesting experiences and meeting new people all the time.

All my love,

Freddie

▶ **Letter from Freddie to Lucy**

21st December

Dear Lucy,

Please try to visit my mum and dad this Christmas. Give them a big hug from me.

I sent them a postcard yesterday. I told them I was in England for a holiday at Christmas and I was watching everyone do their Christmas shopping. I wasn't completely lying to them. But I couldn't tell them the truth. I came to England illegally ten days ago.

I came in the back of a lorry. I would never have done it on my own, but some older boys helped me. We climbed into the lorry when the driver wasn't looking, then we hid behind some boxes. We had to stay as quiet as possible and hope that the police wouldn't check the back of the lorry. I was so afraid I thought I was going to be sick. Each time the lorry stopped moving, my heart was going so quickly I could hear it banging in my head. But nobody found us, not even when we finally arrived. It was dark and easy just to jump out of the lorry. Then we all ran away as fast as we could.

I feel like a criminal. Well, I *am* a criminal. I suppose I'm as bad as Mr Crane now. I had such a lovely dream. But it has become a nightmare – a nightmare from which I may never wake up.

I shouldn't have come here. I know that now. Everything's just the same here as it was before. I'm still alone. I'm still afraid. The only difference is that I'm so cold I feel like my hands and feet have turned to ice.

I've got one last chance to make things better. If I could just make it to London …

Freddie

► **Report from Tower Bridge Hospital**

30th January

Patient information: Young boy, aged approximately fourteen or fifteen. Suffered violent attack

Name: Not known

Address: Not known

Date of Birth: Not known   **Nationality:** Not known

Other details: None

Injuries: Patient unconscious on arrival. Head injuries. Bad cuts to head and upper body. Left arm – broken

Treatment[14]: Stitches in arm, head. Surgery to left arm. Keep in hospital for tests

Other action: We cannot contact any family as we know nothing about this child. There was a business card of a journalist in his pocket. We will phone the journalist for further information. A report has been sent to the police and child support services.

► **Email from Tower Bridge Hospital**
Date: 6th February
From: Hospital Child Support
To: Trevor Baynham
Subject: Patient information

Mr Baynham,

Thank you for all your help with Freddie. He's going to need a lot of support over the next few months, so he's lucky to have you by his side.

I understand that you're contacting government departments and other support organisations. While they are helping Freddie with advice, education and somewhere to stay, we will continue to help him with his health problems.
This boy has suffered terribly since he left his country. He has been badly affected by the terrifying things that have happened to him, including the attack last week.

Freddie is exhausted and in extreme pain, but the physical pain will be easier to take care of than the painful memories.
Sincerely,
Dr Lucy Spencer

► **Freddie's diary**
7th February
I don't know what's happening to me. Nothing seems real. There are too many sad and frightening thoughts inside my head. I can't let them all out. I can't tell people.

Dr Spencer told me I should write things down in this book instead. She says it will help me to get better. How can writing make me feel better? And writing is painful with a broken arm!

8th February

I've been frightened and alone for months. And I've changed. I'm not the same boy I was a year ago. The old Freddie has disappeared and I don't know where he's gone. I don't know who I am any more. I used to be a good boy, but I became a criminal and did very bad things. I begged in the street and I sometimes stole food. Then I came to England illegally and now I'm frightened that the police will lock me up.

11th February

Mr Baynham spoke to my uncle last night. He said that my uncle cried when he heard I was safe. He already knew that I was in trouble because Lucy had told him. He's bringing Mum and Dad to his house tonight so I can talk to them on the phone.

I want to speak to Mum and Dad again, I really do, but I don't think I can. I feel guilty because I've lost all their money and lied to them. They knew the old Freddie – the good Freddie. They'll want to talk to him, not me.

▶ **Letters from Freddie**

12th February

Dear Mum and Dad,

I was so happy to hear your voices on the phone yesterday. I'm sorry I couldn't say anything, but I couldn't stop crying. I've missed you so much. And I'm just so sorry – sorry you lost all your money, sorry that I lied to you and sorry that you've been so worried about me.

The doctors say I'm slowly improving, but it could take many months before I'm fully well again. I believe them. At the moment I feel like I'm an old man, not a young boy. My body hurts, I feel weak and I've always got a headache. But after speaking to you, I feel peaceful and happy for the first time in months.

Please don't worry about me. Mr Baynham's a good man, not like Mr Crane. You can trust him and he's really taking care of me.

Love,

Freddie

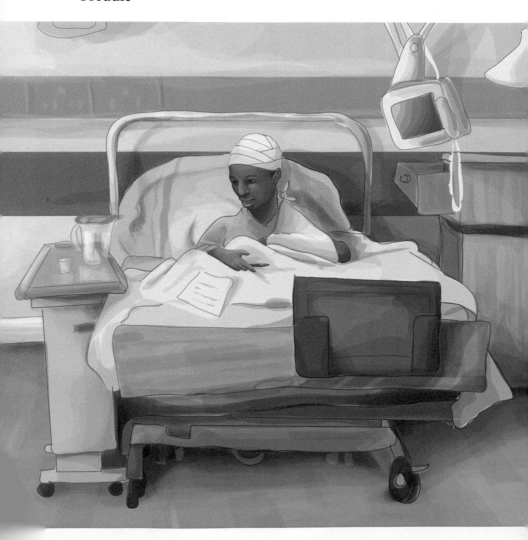

16th February

Dear Lucy,

I don't know what would have happened to me if the doctors hadn't found Mr Baynham's business card in my pocket. And I'm so happy that he was willing to help. He came to visit me in hospital, then he immediately started making lots of phone calls. He says that journalists are like detectives. That's how he was able to get hold of your dad's mobile number. I'm sorry I asked you to tell lies, Lucy. But well done for being sensible[15] and telling the adults everything. It was the right thing to do.

Freddie

20th February

Dear Mum and Dad,

It's very busy here. Lots of people are coming to the hospital to talk to me. They all ask me the same questions, so it's a bit boring at times.

Mr Baynham's still making phone calls and signing piles of papers now too. I don't always understand what's happening, but he keeps telling me that everything's going to be all right. I'm not in trouble.

He has been in touch with an organisation that helps young people who arrive in the UK on their own. They're going to look after me. I'm going to stay in a house with some other boys who've been separated from their families.

I'm looking forward to leaving the hospital, although I'll have to come back twice a week for treatment.

17th April

Dear Mum and Dad,

My new house is very big. There are twelve boys and three adults living here. The adults are very kind and we can talk to them about our problems if we want to. I'm sharing a room with a boy who's about the same age as me. And guess what, Mum? I'm learning to cook and I have to keep my room tidy!

Mr Baynham visits me regularly when he's not working. And I'm starting school next week. I promise I'll work really hard and try to make you proud of me.

Love,

Freddie

22nd May

Dear Lucy,

Thanks for your letter. Now that I've got an actual address, you can write to me as often as you want.

Yes, I like living in London, especially now that the weather is getting warmer! I can already speak a little bit of English because we learned it at school. I just wish I'd listened more in class, though. I was usually too busy thinking about sport. I'm suffering for it now because I have to go to special English classes.

Anyway, there are some nice children in the class. One of the girls is called Safi. She looks about twelve, the same age as you, but her English is so much better than mine! It's so embarrassing! She's a good kid and we spend a lot of time together. She reminds me of you. I think it's because she jokes with me – she's always telling me that I can't spell! We laugh a lot together, but I do feel sorry for her. I miss my family very much, but at least I know that I'll see you all again. But little Safi's father and brother were killed! Isn't that terrible? She's only a child and she's suffered so much.

I'm feeling tired now, so I'd better go to sleep. It still feels good to have my own bed.

Freddie

1st June

Dear Mum and Dad,

I've started my own football team! Don't worry, Mum, I checked with my doctor first. He said the exercise would be good for me. I'm the captain and I play with some boys from my house and my English class. We do our training at the community centre. We're not good enough to play in competitions yet, but we're having great fun. We just need to think of a name for our team.

Freddie

15th July

Dear Lucy,

I never thought I could have such a good birthday without you all. I wasn't really looking forward to it, but it was wonderful. And I got so many presents, even though I don't know many people here.

Last year I got money for my birthday. Do you remember? I thought it was the best present ever. But I was wrong. This year I got two very special presents that I'll always remember. The first was from Safi – it's just an old bag in the shape of an elephant but, believe me, it's the most generous present I've ever received. The second was a hug from Safi's mother – it's just what I needed.

Freddie

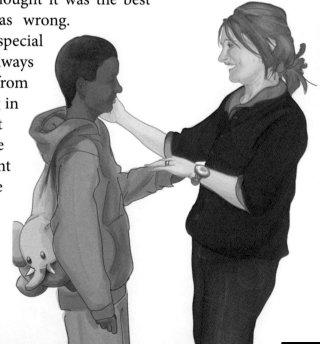

Dear Mum and Dad,

Thank you for my birthday card. I missed you all today, but people here have been very kind to me.

Guess what my teacher gave me as a birthday present? You'll never believe it! It was the biggest parcel I've ever seen and I couldn't think what was inside. When I opened it up, though, I was so shocked, I couldn't speak. It was a football kit for my team! We now have our own football shirts and shorts and boots. What an amazing present! I didn't know what to say.

'Just keep scoring goals, Freddie,' she said to me. 'That will be thanks enough for me.'

So, that's what I'm going to do.

Love,

Freddie

LOOKING BACK

1 Check your answers to *Looking forward* on page 33.

ACTIVITIES

2 Complete the sentences with the words in the box.

Lucy	villagers	Freddie (x2)	Freddie's parents
Trevor	Mr Crane (x2)		

1   *Freddie* wants to become a famous footballer.

2   .... searches for good young football players.

3   .... don't seem interested in the football academy.

4   Some .... collect money for Freddie's training.

5   .... wants to go to the football academy.

6   .... takes the 3,000 euros and disappears.

7   .... gives Freddie some money and a business card.

8   .... is the person Freddie writes to about his problems.

3 Underline the correct words in each sentence.

1   Freddie lives in a *football academy* / <u>*small village.*</u>

2   Freddie dreams of becoming famous because he wants to *be rich* / *look after his parents*.

3   The hotel manager tells Freddie to leave because he *has no money* / *is alone*.

4   Freddie asks Trevor to *find his parents for him* / *let him stay at his house*.

5   His condition *improves* / *gets worse* at the hospital.

6   Safi's mum gives Freddie *a bag* / *a hug* for his birthday.

56

4 What do the underlined words refer to in these sentences from the text?

1 When I think about <u>this</u> I get very excited. (page 34)
   becoming a professional footballer

2 I've heard that <u>this</u> is where he sends the best young football players. (page 35) ....

3 But I couldn't tell <u>them</u> the truth. (page 46)
   ....

4 She says <u>it</u> will help me to get better. (page 48)
   ....

5 I wasn't really looking forward to <u>it</u>, but it was wonderful. (page 53) ....

5 Answer the questions.

1 Why can't Freddie's parents send him to a foreign country?
   ....

2 Why does Freddie write in his diary that he became a criminal?
   ....

3 How does Safi make Freddie think of Lucy?
   ....

4 How is Freddie's party in his home country different from the one in the UK?
   ....
   ....

LOOKING FORWARD

• •

6 Tick (✓) what you think happens in the next chapter.
1 Safi gives up writing. ☐
2 Freddie and Safi stop being friends. ☐

Chapter 4

The Student

World One

► **Email from Maya to her ex-teacher in her home country**
Date: 15th June
From: Maya
To: Janice Tucker
Subject: Thank you

Dear Mrs Tucker,

I wanted to thank you for all your help over the past year. I'm very happy that I passed my exams, but I still can't believe that I got the best results in the university! I can't wait to tell my dad. He's away on business at the moment, as usual, but I'll tell him tonight when he rings me. I know he'll be proud of me.

I wouldn't have done so well without your help. You've taught me so much and made me feel so much better about myself. I'd really like to be a teacher too so that I can make somebody else feel just the way I feel now – happy and confident.

Thank you again for everything.

Maya

► **Email from Maya's ex-teacher**
Date: 17th June
From: Janice Tucker
To: Maya
Subject: Thank you too

Dear Maya,

Thank you for your email and the beautiful flowers – they arrived this morning.

I wasn't surprised to hear that you achieved such excellent results. You've been my best student during the last three years. You've worked extremely hard, listened carefully during classes and done lots of extra practice in your own time. You deserve[16] your achievement.

I think you'd be a wonderful teacher. You're kind and patient and very good with people. Here's an idea. Why don't you train to be an English teacher and why not go to England to study? You already speak the language well and you once told me you'd love to spend some time in the UK. It would be hard work, but I'm confident that you'd do well.

Stay in touch.

Janice Tucker

▶ **Email from Maya's father**

Date: 30th June

From: Dad

To: Maya

Subject: Congratulations!

My darling daughter,

Well done! I'm so happy that you've achieved such excellent results. The best results in the university!

I am so proud of you, darling. You're everything to me. Since your mum died, things have been so difficult at times, I know. But you're the most important thing in my life and I only want the best for you. I know you found it hard to leave home and your friends to go to university. Now you can see that your daddy was right! It was the best university that money could buy and you have had the best education possible. These results show that I did the right thing.

Sorry I can't be with you at the moment, but I'm thinking of you. The business is hard work at the moment and I'm away a lot, I know, but I need to work hard. I need to make sure you have everything you want. I know you understand.

I'm glad you want to go abroad to continue your studies. We'll talk about it when I come back home for your graduation ceremony[17].

All my love,

Dad

► **Letters from Maya's father**

15th July

My darling Maya,

I'm sorry that I won't be able to get to your graduation ceremony. I really wanted to see you get your degree[18], but I've got a very important business meeting. I can't cancel it. I know you understand.

I hope you like this necklace – it's a small present to show you how much I love you. Wear it on your special day so you know that I'm thinking of you. You're always in my thoughts and in my heart, my darling daughter. Remember that!

20th August

Thank you for sending me the photos of your graduation ceremony, darling. You look beautiful and intelligent. I'm glad you liked the necklace. It was very expensive – you deserve the best because you *are* the best.

Now for a surprise! I agree that it's a good idea for you to go abroad and continue your studies in the UK. That way you can improve your English while you're studying. So I've decided to pay for you to do a higher degree in Business Studies in London, England. Then you can come back here and be my assistant. I'll teach you all about the company because one day I'll be old and you'll have to take over the family business. You'll be just like your father – a leader in the business world. Won't that be exciting?

Go and see my sales manager at Head Office. He's got all the information about the course. I know that you'll continue to work just as hard on your Business Studies course as you did on your language degree, and be the best student there too.
Love,
Daddy

► **Email from Maya to her ex-teacher**
Date: 19th October
From: Maya
To: Janice Tucker
Subject: London

I've been at university in London for three weeks now. It's everything I'd hoped it would be – lively, exciting and fun. It's strange, but I feel like I've always known London. Perhaps it's because I've read about it so often. So, even though I miss my country, I don't feel sad. Actually, I feel more confident here than I did at home. Isn't that odd? And there's always so much to do here. I absolutely love it.

The problem is that I hate the Business Studies course. I'm good with words, not numbers. I'm trying really hard but I'm probably the worst student in the class! My father's paid a lot for me to do this course, so I can't tell him that I only got fifty-two percent for my first piece of work, can I?

Anyway, I've already made some good friends and, of course, my English is improving every day. This is mainly because everyone around me is speaking English all the time. But I'd much rather be learning to teach English than learning about business.

The Language Department at this university is excellent. I often use their computers to practise reading and writing English. Students can use the computers for free, which is useful. I go there so often that I've already become friends with the receptionist! She told me that the department does a very good English Language Teaching course. Oh, I'd love to do that. It's much better than boring business. Never mind! One day, perhaps.
Maya

► **Letter from Maya to the university**

15th November

Dear Sir,

Re: Change of course

We recently spoke about my plan to change course, from Business Studies to English Language Teaching.

This letter is to confirm[19] my decision. The cost of the Business Studies course has already been paid for in full, but I would like to use this money to pay for the English Language Teaching course instead.

As I explained, I already have a language degree, so there should be no problem with this move or with the extra coursework I'll need to do over the next few weeks.

Thank you for your help.

Yours faithfully,

Student Number 98457

► **Emails from Maya to her ex-teacher**

Date: 12th December
From: Maya
To: Janice Tucker
Subject: Changes

I've done a terrible thing. I have to tell somebody. I changed my course and didn't tell my dad.

You know how badly I was doing on that business degree course, don't you? I hated every minute of it. I realised that I was trying to be somebody else – not Maya. And I was doing it just to please my dad. That's why I was failing. So I decided it was time to do something that I actually *enjoy* doing.

I'm on the English Language Teaching course now and I love it! I'm getting good results again – for my written work and my teaching. I have to do teaching practice as part of the course. This means I have to teach students in different places and at different levels. My teaching supervisor[20], David, comes to watch me and reports to me on how well I'm doing.

He says I'm a natural teacher. I know he's right. I feel like I'm the real Maya when I'm in front of a class. For the first time in my life I'm doing what *I* want. I feel very naughty but very free at the same time.

I just needed to share this with somebody.

Thanks,

Maya

Date: 20th May
From: Maya
To: Janice Tucker
Subject: Help!

My dad's coming to see me in a few weeks' time. I never thought he'd visit me here in England. Flights are so expensive and he doesn't usually have the time.

I don't know how to tell him what I've done. I know he'll be very disappointed that I want to be a teacher and not a businesswoman. And I'm sure that he'll be extremely angry that I've changed courses without telling him. I haven't lied to him, though. Not really. I just haven't told him the truth. Is that the same thing as lying? I suppose it is.

I might not tell him – not yet, anyway. Thankfully, my classes have finished and I've already handed in my last piece of written work (fifteen thousand words about teaching adults!). I can spend time with Dad but keep him away from the university. My course isn't quite over yet, though, because I have to spend six weeks doing my final teaching practice.

This won't happen until long after Dad goes back home, so I should be safe.

Part of me thinks I shouldn't tell him yet. I'll wait until I've finished every part of my course, then I can show him all my good results when I go back home.

Another part of me thinks I should tell him the truth now. It would be the best thing to do. Perhaps he'll be happy when he sees how well I'm doing.

Maya

PS: Sorry if I sound confused. I thought it might help me to make a decision if I wrote it all down … it hasn't!

▶ **Letter from Maya's father**

6th June

Maya,

When you get this note I'll already be at the airport. I'm taking an early flight home. I wasn't going to start work until next week, but I can't stay here now.

I've seen the results for your final piece of coursework. I wasn't going to open the letter because it had your name on it, but I couldn't help myself. You told me how well you were doing. I just wanted to see your excellent results in writing. Eighty-eight percent! I was so happy.

Then I saw the subject of your coursework: *Teaching English to Adults*. What has this got to do with business, I asked myself? They must have sent the wrong results. So I checked the name of your course on the letter.

Do I need to say any more? Do I? How could you do this to me, Maya? I was going to ring you before I left, but I was so angry I could hardly speak. In fact, I still don't want to talk to you. We've just spent such a lovely week together and you never said a word about any of this to me.

All I've ever wanted was the best for you. I've paid for the best schools, the best colleges and the best universities. You've had all the opportunities in life that other people can only dream of. And how do you repay me? You use my money to train to be a teacher. A teacher, Maya? What were you thinking of?

I've been telling everyone about your Business Studies course. I've told everybody at work that you'll join me next year as my assistant. What will they think if they find out that my selfish daughter has lied to me and cheated?

Don't try to ring me, Maya. I don't want to speak to you at the moment. I need time to decide what to do next. I am so disappointed in you. You're my only child and you've hurt me very badly.

Dad

Deadly earthquake

By Trevor Baynham

 We were all shocked to hear about this morning's huge earthquake. Even though the disaster happened thousands of miles away from us here in the UK, it has affected many people who live in this country. It's important that we realise this.

I have spent the day standing outside the embassy[21] in London. I talked to some of the people who were waiting to find out what had happened to their relatives on the other side of the world. Crowds had made their way to central London to see if the people who work at the embassy could give them more information about the situation.

The problem is the embassy has no more news

than anybody else at the moment. They can't contact anyone for information.

We still do not have a clear picture of what has happened. All we know is that it was a very powerful earthquake in the south of the country and that it happened during the day, while people were at work and at school. There are some reports that many buildings, including businesses, schools and colleges have been badly hit by the earthquake. That's why people here are so worried. If these reports are true, then it's likely that there could be many deaths and injuries.

None of these reports have been confirmed yet and it could be hours before any fresh information is received. But the people won't leave. They feel that the embassy is the only place where they may still get the latest information.

When people realise I'm a journalist, they turn to me for help. They think that I might know something important, but I don't.

Some people come up to me and show me pictures of their sons, daughters, wives and husbands. They ask me to contact journalists in their country to find out what is happening. I try to make them understand that it isn't possible. I try to tell them that I can't find their relatives. I explain that I'm used to providing the news, not waiting for it, so I understand how they feel.

But they either don't understand or they don't believe me – I don't blame them. When people are frightened they don't think logically. It's understandable, but it doesn't make me feel any better that I can't help. I felt particularly helpless when I spoke to a young woman I met today.

She ran towards me and put a photograph in my hand.

'It's my dad. I can't reach him,' she said. 'What should I do? I've been trying to ring him for hours. I keep sending emails too, but I don't get any replies. I couldn't just sit at home by a silent phone, so I

came here. I've even brought this picture with me, in case ... well, I don't know, really. I thought maybe I could give it to someone at the embassy. And perhaps they could send it back to my country.'

She looked at me with

hope in her eyes, but it soon died when she saw the look on my face. She took the photo back.

'But I realise now that nobody can help,' she admitted. 'I just need to speak to him. I need to know he's OK.'

I asked her when she had last seen her father. She was so full of fear that she spoke far too quickly.

'The day before yesterday. He was staying with me. I'm studying here and I got eighty-eight percent in my coursework and he found out, so he wrote me a letter and then he left.'

She suddenly started to cry very loudly. She tried to keep talking through her tears but I couldn't understand her properly. The only words I thought I heard were, 'I'm sorry. I need to tell him that I'm sorry.'

'That's a very good result. I'm sure he's very proud of you!' I said, trying to make her feel better.

But these words just made her cry even more.

'He *was* proud of me,' she replied. 'He was once very proud of me.'

'He *is* proud of you,' I corrected her. 'You mustn't talk about him in the past yet.'

'Thank you,' she smiled through her tears. 'You're very kind. But, you don't understand. You see, he was proud of me once but not now. Now he doesn't want to speak to me. He doesn't even want to hear my voice. But, you see, I need to hear his voice. I really do.'

She held the picture of her father to her chest and closed her eyes. It was as if she believed that if she thought about him hard enough, she could make him appear.

I quietly wished her good luck and left her in the crowd. I completely understood the young lady's fears about her father's safety, but not her belief that he didn't want to talk to her. As I said, when people are frightened they think illogically. And there are a lot of frightened people here at the moment.

▶ **Email from Maya to her father**
Date: 10th June
From: Maya
To: Dad
Subject: Email failure notice
Problem: email wasn't delivered
Reason: unknown email address

My darling Daddy,

Please find a way to let me know you are safe. I LOVE YOU DADDY. AND I AM SO SORRY. I never wanted to hurt you. I'll come back home and be a businesswoman. Teaching was a stupid idea, I know that now. I was just following my dream, but that's all it was – a dream. The reality is that I'm your daughter and I want you to be proud of me again. I'll do everything I can to help you when I get back. Just tell me you're OK. I'm sending this message to both your addresses – home and office. I've tried ringing, but none of the numbers work. Please ring me. I know you said you don't want to talk to me but please ring me. PLEASE.
Maya

▶ **Email from Maya's teaching supervisor**
Date: 15th June
From: David Morgan
To: Maya
Subject: Support

Dear Maya,

I was so sorry to hear about the situation in your country.

I'm sure you're extremely worried about your family and friends. If there's anything I can do to help you, please let me know.

Remember that the university has very good support services. Do contact them if you need any help with money or somewhere to live.

By the way, I was surprised to hear that you've asked the university if you can start a Business Studies course in September. Of course, you must make your own decision, but it would be a good idea if you finished your teaching course first. You have just six weeks of work left and then you'll have your teaching qualification. I'll give you extra time to do your final teaching practice, so please don't worry about that. You can have as much extra time as you need.

I'm here for you if you need to talk.

David Morgan

Teaching Supervisor

▶ **Email from Maya to her teaching supervisor**
Date: 17th June
From: Maya
To: David Morgan (Teaching Supervisor)
Subject: Re: Support

Dear David,

Many thanks for your email and your thoughtful words. Yes, things are very difficult at the moment. I still can't reach my family and friends.

Thank you for offering to let me do my teaching practice at a later date, but I still want to do a Business degree. It's what my father wants me to do. I don't have the money to pay for it at the moment, but my father will send it when he can.

You're very kind to suggest that I talk to the Student Support Services. However, I don't need to do this. My father's got some friends here and they are helping me until my father gets in touch and sends me the money I need.

The people at the embassy have already suggested that I should ask the British government for help. But my father would not be happy if I did that. He always told me it was wrong to take or borrow money from people I don't know.

Thank you again for the offer of help.

Kind regards,

Maya

▶ **Email from Maya's ex-teacher**
Date: 27th July
From: Janice Tucker
To: Maya
Subject: So sorry

Dear Maya,

I'm writing to say that I was so sorry to hear about your father. He was a good man. This is a terrible time in our country's history. So many people have died. We've got a long way to go before we can get back to a normal way of life.

I was one of the lucky ones. I was away from town visiting friends in the north of the country when the earthquake happened. I haven't been able to get back to my part of town but I hear that most of it has been destroyed. Many houses are gone, along with the university. There's nothing left of it.

I'm going back to the north to stay with my friends for the rest of the holiday. I don't know what I'm going to do when term starts again. It's hard to think about work when I'm just glad to be alive.

Janice

Date: 3rd August
From: Maya
To: Janice Tucker
Subject: RE: So sorry

   Well, I'm not glad to be alive. My father was angry with me before he died and said he didn't want to speak to me. I loved him so much and he was disappointed in me. My heart is broken.

   I've only got a few hundred pounds left in my bank now, so I've had to move out of my flat. I now have to rent a room in a house with some of my student friends. Life is hard.

   The sales manager at my father's business contacted me recently. The business is now mine, as well as my father's money. But, of course, there is no business at the moment. As you said in your email, the buildings have all disappeared. I really don't know what to do.

Maya

► **Email from Maya's ex-teacher**
Date: 12th August
From: Janice Tucker
To: Maya
Subject: Be optimistic

Maya,

I know you're going through a very bad time, but please try not to be so pessimistic. Times are hard for many of us at the moment.

I understand that you miss your father very much, but you must remember that he loved you and was very proud of you. One small argument can never change that.

You're much luckier than many, Maya. You've got money, friends and somewhere to live. You can do something good with your life.

Janice

► **Email from Maya to her ex-teacher**
Date: 26th September
From: Maya
To: Janice Tucker
Subject: Confused

Dear Janice,

There's so much that I don't understand at the moment. My father's friends have introduced me to insurance companies and lawyers, but I spend most of my time talking to the sales manager of my father's business. He's a good man and I trust him. He lost his wife and son in the earthquake. I think it is important that he doesn't lose his job too. He's honest and he understands the business.

I want to do what my father asked me to do, I really do. I know he wanted me to take over his business, but I don't know where to start. I couldn't be a company director or a manager. I wasn't even looking forward to being an assistant! I just want to teach. There, I've said it! I just want to teach. Is that so wrong?

Maya

► **Email from Maya's ex-teacher**
Date: 5th October
From: Janice Tucker
To: Maya
Subject: Re: Confused

Dear Maya,

You did everything your father asked of you. You did all you could to please him. You did what he thought was right for you. Now you must do what you know is right for you.

If this disaster has taught me anything, it's that life is too short, so we must live it well. Your father did that. He did what he was good at and he was the best businessman he could be. Now you must be the best teacher you can be.

Follow your dreams.

Love,

Janice

► **Email from Maya's teaching supervisor**
Date: 11th November
From: David Morgan
To: Maya
Subject: Teaching Practice

Dear Maya,

So good to hear from you. I'm very pleased that you're going to finish your teaching course. You were one of our best students last year. I know you've made the right decision.

I understand that you still have lots of things to organise with your father's business, so I'll try to arrange your final teaching practice for March or April next year. Leave everything to me. I'll email you again soon.

Regards,

David

▶ **Emails from Maya to her ex-teacher**
Date: 28th February
From: Maya
To: Janice Tucker
Subject: Teaching Practice

I'm starting my final teaching practice in April. My teaching supervisor has arranged it for me. I'm not very happy about it, though. Do you know where I'm going to teach? In an old community centre in a very poor part of London.

I went there recently to have a look around. It hasn't got any books or computers. It hasn't even got a board to write on. There's nothing except a few tables and chairs. And I'm going to have to teach teenagers, many of whom are refugees. They're all under eighteen and they all need extra help with their English. I was hoping to teach adults – college students or university students – not teenagers with problems. I really don't think I want to do this.

Maya

Date: 30th April
From: Maya
To: Janice Tucker
Subject: Problems

My first week of teaching practice is over. I'm so pleased I only have five more weeks to go. I hate it. These teenagers are very difficult to teach. They've got lots of problems. Some of them are so nervous they won't say anything. Some don't listen properly. A few of them look like they haven't slept for weeks. Many of them have been sent to me by their schools for extra lessons, so they obviously don't want to be here. And neither do I. I've had a very bad year. I've lost my home and my dad. I've had enough pain and difficulty in my life, so I'm not ready to share theirs as well.
Maya

Date: 25th May
From: Maya
To: Janice Tucker
Subject: Sorry

Dear Janice,

I'm not surprised you didn't reply to my last email. I've just read it again and I feel embarrassed.

I've been so selfish and unkind. You were right to remind me how lucky I was last year. I didn't believe you then but I do now. The teenagers in my class finally made me realise this.

I remember when I asked one of the young girls, Safi, a very simple question one day.

'Do you have any brothers or sisters?'

She said 'No.'

'Me neither,' I said. 'Tell me about your mother and father.'

'Well, there's just me and my mum,' she replied. 'My father and my brother are dead.'

'Oh, I'm sorry, Safi,' I said. 'It seems we have a lot in common. My father is dead too. But you've got your mother though, haven't you?' I said, trying to make her feel better. 'My mother died when I was a child.'

For one moment, she looked hopeful. 'Yes, I am lucky, aren't I?' she said. 'I'm so sorry about your mother and father. Did your neighbours kill them? My neighbours killed my father and my brother. They took them from the house and shot them.'

I was so shocked, I didn't know what to say, so I turned to another student, Freddie, and asked him to tell me about his house.

'I used to live in a house with my family,' he told me. 'I don't have a house now. I have only a room in a house.'

'Me too,' I told him. 'I used to have a big house in my country and a lovely flat here, but now I live in a very small room in a house with three other people. But we're very lucky to have a room, aren't we?'

'Yes, I feel very lucky,' he replied with a smile. 'There are twelve people in my house and I share my room with another boy. I had no house at all for many months because I was living on the street, so I had to sleep on the street or in the park. People used to shout at me. Some people were violent. It was very dangerous. I had to spend weeks in hospital because a group of people attacked me.'

That's when I stopped feeling sorry for myself and started to realise how lucky I was. It's also when I stopped being a student and really started to be a teacher.

Love, Maya

Date: 18th June
From: Maya
To: Janice Tucker
Subject: Thank you

It was so good to hear from you again. I'm glad you haven't stopped emailing me!

I'm much happier now. I asked the community centre if I could continue teaching there even though my teaching practice had finished. I couldn't leave after just six weeks, could I? Those kids needed me – not just to teach them English but to help them to know they were not alone. They've had so much change in their young lives and I do understand a little bit about their suffering. It's amazing though – I wanted to help them, but they helped me instead.

Freddie and Safi got prizes last week, by the way. They were so pleased that they couldn't stop laughing. Soon I was laughing with them. It was the first time I'd laughed since Dad died and it felt so good. Do you know why? Because at that moment, I realised that I'd made my students feel the same way you made me feel – happy and confident.

Do you remember when I first told you that this was why I wanted to teach? It was a long time ago, wasn't it? It seems like a different world. Well, it was a different world, but this one's starting to look a little better than it once did.

Love,

Maya

► **Page from Maya's university graduation book**

QUALIFICATION: English Language Teaching Degree

FUTURE PLANS: Maya has lots of very exciting plans for the future. Her home country suffered badly in the earthquake last year and she wants to help rebuild her father's business. She has regular meetings with the new company director. She is looking forward to working with him until normal business can begin again. She is very happy with her excellent degree results. She already has a job teaching English in a local community centre and she has just been invited to become one of the centre managers. Maya knows that her father would have been very proud of her success. She is really looking forward to this new chapter in her life.

LOOKING BACK

●●●

1 Check your answers to *Looking forward* on page 57.

ACTIVITIES

●●●

2 Are the sentences true (*T*) or false (*F*)?

1 Maya sent her teacher chocolates to thank her. ☐F
2 Her father wants her to study to become a teacher. ☐
3 Maya got an expensive present for her graduation. ☐
4 She wants to do a degree in Business Studies. ☐
5 A terrible natural disaster hit Maya's country. ☐
6 Janice Tucker was saved because she had to go to the north of the country that day. ☐
7 Maya always loved working at the community centre. ☐

3 <u>Underline</u> the correct words in each sentence.

1 Maya gets very good grades *at university* / *in Business Studies*.
2 Janice Tucker suggests that Maya should study *business* / *teaching*.
3 Maya's father *agrees* / *disagrees* with her decision to change course at university.
4 The earthquake hit when people were *at work* / *in bed* and destroyed many buildings in Maya's country.
5 Safi lives with her *mother* / *father*.
6 Maya's dad was killed by *the neighbours* / *a natural disaster*.
7 Freddie lives in a big *house* / *room*.

4 What do the underlined words refer to in these sentences from the text?

1 It would be hard work, (page 59) *studying in the uk*

2 It's everything I'd hoped it would be (page 62)

....

3 I often use their computers (page 62) ....

4 Another part of me thinks I should tell him the truth now. (page 65) ....

5 I try to make them understand that it isn't possible. (page 67)

....

6 I'm not ready to share theirs as well. (page 77)

....

5 Answer the questions.

1 Why doesn't Maya's father go to her graduation ceremony?

....

2 What does Maya's father want her to do in the UK?

....

3 Why is Maya's father upset with her?

....

LOOKING FORWARD

6 What do you think happens in the final chapter? Answer the questions.

1 Do Safi, Freddie and Maya get used to life in the UK?

....

2 Does Trevor see Safi, Freddie and Maya again?

....

3 Does Freddie return to his home country?

....

Chapter 5

A World of Opportunities

Now you know a little bit more about the schoolgirl, the footballer and the student – and not just their names. You've shared their hopes, dreams and happiness in World One. You've travelled with them through the danger, fear and sadness in the news reports. You've watched them face many changes and problems in World Two. So, I thought you'd like to find out what they're doing now.

I visited a community centre in London earlier today. It's in one of the poorer areas of town and the building is old and rather ugly. Outside it looks like an ordinary building, just like all the others around it. But inside extraordinary things are happening. And I'm happy to say that our three new friends are very much part of these things.

The first person I met when I arrived was Maya, who is now one of the centre managers. She had agreed to give me a tour of the centre. And it soon became obvious that she had a lot to tell me about it.

First I asked her how she became involved with the centre. 'Well, I started teaching English here,' Maya began. 'It was only going to be for six weeks but I stayed. I must admit that I didn't like it when I first came here. But the people here welcomed me and my students warmly, so I soon felt comfortable here. I realised that people were the heart of this centre. They didn't have much money, so they couldn't improve the building, but they were loving and kind and worked hard to keep it open.

Now I'm happy to be able to help them. When I arrived, I contacted local businesses and other important people in the area and asked them to help us. We soon had enough money to develop the centre and add to its activities. Come and see.'

She gave me a wide smile.

'I manage education here. We provide classes in languages, cooking, drawing, music and many other subjects. The other centre managers look after the advice centre, computer centre, sports centre and the kitchen and dining area. We've also got lots of volunteers working here. They don't get any money for their work. They're happy to work at the centre without pay because they believe they're helping the community. It's amazing to see people from so many different countries and cultures working together. They're making friends and learning about each other at the same time.'

I reminded Maya of our first meeting outside the embassy and how she was worried about what her father thought of her. I told her that I believed her father would be very proud of what she was doing now, not only for the centre, but also for her students. Her face went a little red and her eyes became cloudy for a few seconds. I was worried that I'd made her feel sad again, but then she smiled.

'Thank you, Trevor. You're very kind. And I agree. I think he would be very proud of me. I was surprised to discover that I'm actually a very good businesswoman, just like my father said I would be.'

'So, you've stopped teaching then?' I asked.

'Absolutely not!' she replied. 'I make sure that I've always got time to teach. It's what I do best.'

Maya then led me down a narrow corridor as she talked happily about the centre.

'There used to be nothing for young people to do around here,' she explained to me. 'They used to get very bored. But now, we can offer them all kinds of activities, including sport.'

We had reached the end of the corridor and were now standing in front of two huge doors.

'There used to be an old garage next to the community centre. We bought it, and just look at it now!'

She opened the doors wide and in front of me was a big sports centre, full of people having fun.

'Sports activities are very popular, as you can see. We started with just a couple of exercise classes and now we have a different class every day. We also do football training here. Freddie's a big help with this. Where's Freddie?'

'I'll go and get him,' said one of the volunteers.

'But, of course, you know him even better than I do,' Maya remembered. 'He's the manager of our under 11s team, as well as playing in the 12–18 team. He might also be our very own superstar! He's just been invited to train with a professional football team.'

I looked round and Freddie was behind me, smiling his brightest smile. He looked very excited.

'Well, I'm not a superstar yet!' he joked. 'I'll be training with lots of other people. Our local football club runs courses for boys in a similar situation to me. One of their coaches has been here a few times to watch me play and he thinks I'm good enough to join the course. So, you never know. If I do well, I might get the chance to train at a *real* football academy!'

I told Freddie that I'd give him all the help I could.

'Thank you,' said Freddie. 'And I've got someone else to give me support too.' He turned and introduced me to a tall, grey-haired man. He had the same eyes and smile as Freddie. I knew immediately who he was.

'You're Freddie's father!' I said. 'We've spoken on the phone many times. It's good to finally meet you.'

'And I'm extremely happy to meet you, Trevor,' he replied. 'Thank you so much for looking after my boy.'

And we hugged as if we had known each other for ever.

A little later, Maya took me to see the kitchen and dining room at the centre.

'This is where our lunches are prepared,' she told me. 'Our cooked lunches are different every day because we use recipes from different countries, don't we, Mrs P?'

'Yes and some of them are better than others, aren't they, Maya?' a voice called back from the kitchen. It was Safi's mum and she was laughing as she came out to greet us.

Maya smiled back. 'Yes. I admit that some recipes are a bit odd! Anyway, let me introduce you to Mr Baynham.'

'Trevor and I already know each other,' said Safi's mum, as she came forward to shake my hand. 'Things have changed a lot since our first meeting, as you know. Safi and I live in a little flat near here now. I come to the centre as often as I can. I enjoy helping in the kitchen and meeting other people. It's been so good for me to make new friends. Life still isn't easy and I often feel very sad when I think about how my life used to be. But I'm much happier now than I was and so is Safi.'

'Where is Safi?' I asked.

'Oh, she'll probably be in the garden,' Safi's mum replied. 'She spends a lot of time there because it reminds her of home. Or she might be in the library. You know what she's like – she usually has her head in a book!'

Maya looked at her watch. 'You're right. She'll be in the library. Her writing class has just finished and she always does her homework in the library.'

'Ah, your daughter, the writer!' I said. 'She's still practising, then?'

'Every day, Trevor. Just like her teacher told her to do when she gave her the diary. She's the best student in her writing class, you know. I'm so proud of her. Go and see her. I know she'll be pleased to see you. '

As I left the two women laughing and joking together I had a warm feeling inside. Safi's mum was right. Life here still wasn't easy, but it was much better now that she'd made some friends.

I walked quietly into the library and I could see Safi sitting at a table, with books all around her.

'Hi, Safi,' I whispered.

Safi looked up from her books and gave me a beautiful smile. Then she stood up and ran over to me.

'Your mum says you're top of the class again. Is that right?' I asked.

'Yes, I am. Isn't that brilliant? Maya has helped me so much that I can now write my poems in English. They're only simple and I need to use my dictionary, but it's still amazing. When I first came here I didn't understand a word.'

'What about your diary?' I asked

'Oh yes, my diary.'

She suddenly looked very serious. For one awful moment,

I saw the dark look in her eyes that I'd seen when I first met her. Then, thankfully, she smiled again.

'I think that diary saved my life, you know. I wrote all my secret thoughts in there. Sometimes it seemed like my only friend. Now I have real friends, but I still write in my diary. And I still write it in my own language. It's very important that I remember my language, especially as the government tried to get rid of it.'

'So, do you still dream of being a writer?' I asked her.

'I don't have to dream. I *am* a writer,' she replied. 'Here, have a copy of my new poem. You might want to put it in your book.'

And she was right. I do.

Poem

Two Worlds

I'm caught between two worlds
    Then and Now
    I don't know how
    I moved from living there
    to feeling lonely here
I'm caught between two worlds
    Safe and Lost
    I paid the cost
    Of leaving loved ones there
    and meeting strangers here
I'm caught between two worlds
    Happy and Sad
    I lost what I had
    I left my old self there
    and couldn't bring her here
I'm caught between two worlds
    Sunshine and Rain
    It's not a game
    I had to wave goodbye to there
    and say hello to here
I'm caught between two worlds
    Old and New
    It's up to you
    To help me move from missing there
    to feeling welcome here

LOOKING BACK

1 Check your answers to *Looking forward* on page 83.

ACTIVITIES

2 Complete the summary of Chapter 5 with the words in the box.

> Safi's mum   Trevor (x3)
> Maya   Freddie   Safi

¹ *Trevor* goes to the community centre where ² .... works as a manager and a teacher. Here ³ .... meets all the people he has been helping. ⁴ .... is coaching the football team at the centre and ⁵ .... is helping in the kitchen. ⁶ .... has become very good at English and she still writes in her diary. She also writes poetry now and ⁷ .... decides to include one of her poems in his book.

3 Underline the correct words in each sentence.

1 Trevor visits the *football academy / community centre.*
2 The first person he talks to is *Maya / Freddie.*
3 When Maya first came to the centre people *disliked / were friendly towards* her.
4 Maya is happy because she can *help / meet* people at the centre.
5 Maya believes her father would be *disappointed in her / proud of her.*
6 Safi's writes poems in *her own language / English.*

4 Match the two parts of the sentences.

1 Although Safi, Freddie and Maya are not in their home countries, [c]

2 Maya is a successful teacher, ☐

3 Freddie manages the children's football team, ☐

4 Freddie's dad is very happy to meet Trevor ☐

5 Safi is top of her class ☐

6 Safi's mum can now help with the kitchen ☐

7 Maya, Safi and Freddie are happy now ☐

a while playing for the older boys' team.

b because he's helped his son.

c they feel comfortable in their new home.

d because they can help other people.

e because Maya has helped her.

f because she isn't as sad any more.

g but works as a centre manager as well.

5 Answer the questions.

1 What does Trevor mean by World One?

....

2 What does Trevor mean by World Two?

....

3 Where is the community centre?

....

4 What does Maya think is surprising about the volunteers?

....

5 Why does Safi tell Trevor that the diary saved her life?

....

Glossary

[1]**earthquake** (page 5) *noun*   a sudden movement of the Earth's surface, which often causes terrible damage

[2]**shocked** (page 6) *verb*   to feel upset or surprised

[3]**refugee** (page 6) *noun*   someone who has been made to leave their country, especially because of a war or natural disaster

[4]**support** (page 7) *noun*   help or encouragement

[5]**proud** (page 11) *adjective*   when you feel very pleased about something you have done

[6]**contact** (page 14) *verb*   to telephone someone or write to them

[7]**sensitive** (page 15) *adjective*   easily upset by the things people say or do

[8]**interpreter** (page 19) *noun*   someone whose job is to change what someone else is saying into another language

[9]**attack** (page 20) *verb*   to use violence to hurt or damage someone or something

[10]**proper** (page 23) *adjective*   suitable for someone

[11]**community centre** (page 25) *noun*   a place where people who live in an area can meet together to play sport, go to classes, etc

[12]**agent** (page 35) *noun*   someone whose job is to take care of business for someone else

[13]**illegally** (page 43) *adverb*   not allowed by law

[14]**treatment** (page 47) *noun*   something which you do to give care to someone who is ill or hurt, especially something suggested or done by a doctor

[15]**sensible** (page 51) *adjective*   showing good judgement

[16]**deserve** (page 59) *noun*   to earn or receive something because of the way you have behaved or the qualities you have

[17]**graduation ceremony** (page 60) *noun*   an important event that takes place when you receive a **degree** for completing your university course

[18]**degree** (page 60) *noun*   a qualification given for completing a university course

[19]**confirm** (page 63) *verb*   to say or show that something is true

[20]**supervisor** (page 64) *noun*   someone who watches a person or activity and makes certain that everything is done correctly, safely, etc

[21]**embassy** (page 66) *noun*   the building where a group of people work who represent their country in a foreign country